3 Month in June 7, 1988   7 Month

CONTENTS

Cover:
Closeup of the head of a Cockatiel. Photo by Dr. Gerald R. Allen.

Front endpapers: photo by Dr. Herbert R. Axelrod
Back endpapers: photo by Harry V. Lacey

Dedicated to our sons, Tony and Mark.

t.f.h.

ISBN 0-87666-757-4

Distributed in the U.S. by T.F.H. Publications, Inc., 211 West Sylvania Avenue, PO Box 427, Neptune, NJ 07753; in England by T.F.H. (Gt. Britain) Ltd., 13 Nutley Lane, Reigate, Surrey; in Canada to the pet trade by Rolf C. Hagen Ltd., 3225 Sartelon Street, Montreal 382, Quebec; in Southeast Asia by Y.W. Ong, 9 Lorong 36 Geylang, Singapore 14; in Australia and the South Pacific by Pet Imports Pty. Ltd., P.O. Box 149, Brookvale 2100, N.S.W. Australia; in South Africa by Valid Agencies, P.O. Box 51901, Randburg 2125 South Africa. Published by T.F.H. Publications, Inc., Ltd, the British Crown Colony of Hong Kong.

all bout cockatiels

dr. gerald r. allen and connie j. allen

Cockatoos are the largest of all the Australian parrots and parrot-like birds. This beautiful specimen is also called the Galah or Rose-Breasted Cockatoo, *Eolophus roseicapillus*. Photo by Dr. Gerald R. Allen.

The lorikeets are represented in Australia by only six species. This is the Coconut Lory. Photo by Dr. Gerald R. Allen.

INTRODUCTION

It was slightly over four years ago that we first set foot on the shores of Australia. We had been cruising around New Guinea and various islands in the Solomon Sea aboard a small biological research vessel. Our first port of call on the Australian island continent was Cairns, a lovely little tourist town nestled between the sea and rain forest covered slopes of far north Queensland. One of our first and most lasting impressions of our introduction to Australia was the sight of a flock of wild Rainbow Lorikeets, chattering loudly as they devoured nectar from the blossoms of a large tree. One has to see this magnificent bird in the wilds to truly appreciate it. We watched, completely enthralled by their fascinating acrobatics and could scarcely believe the beauty of the bright colored plumage, a combination of neon blue, green, red and yellow. This was our introduction to Australian parrots and what began as a casual moment of interest has gradually become a completely absorbing hobby.

We soon discovered there is a host of parrots native to Australia. . .52 species to be exact. Their variety is truly incredible. One normally thinks of parrots as being inhabitants of tropical jungles. In Australia this is true to a limited extent. There are several species such as the Rainbow Lorikeet, Varied Lorikeet, Red Cheek Parrot, and Palm Cockatoo which are primarily restricted to the northern rain forests. However, other Australian parrots are adapted to a wide variety of habitat conditions. Indeed there are parrots to be found in nearly every conceivable situation including the vicinity of large cities and even along the seashore of rocky islets (the domain of the Rock Parrot, *Neophema petrophila*). Perhaps the most interesting species are those which inhabit the arid interior, which covers many thousands of square miles. This is an inhospitable terrain with little water and mostly low scrubby desert vegetation. The parrots which live here are generally nomadic, settling for a while following periodic rain showers and then moving on when the local water supply has diminished. The arid regions contain occa-

The Cockatiel, *Nymphicus hollandicus*, is one of the world's favorite bird pets. Photo by Connie J. Allen.

The Budgerigar, *Melopsittacus undulatus,* is the best known of the 52 psittacines from Australia. It inhabits the arid interior. (Below) The family Psittacidae is the largest group of Australian psittacines. This is Bourke's Parrot (*Neophema bourkii*). It is found in the arid regions of central and western Australia. Photo by Dr. Gerald R. Allen.

The crest, which is erectile, is most highly developed in species belonging to the genus *Cacatua*. This is the prized Major Mitchell Cockatoo, *Cacatua leadbeateri*. Photo by Dr. Gerald Allen.

sional eucalypt-lined streams which are often dry, but when flowing provide a breeding oasis for the nomadic parrots. The species which successfully dwell under these marginal conditions are perhaps the most rugged and adaptive of all parrots. Therefore it is not surprising that two of these, the Budgerigar and Cockatiel, have established a reputation of being the most durable and most easily bred parrot-like birds kept in captivity.

After several months in Australia we eventually decided to settle there permanently and almost immediately began taking a serious interest in Australian wildlife, particularly the psittacine fauna. Soon after moving to Sydney we began keeping different parrot-like birds in captivity. At one time or another we had various cockatoos, rosellas, lorikeets, and Cockatiels. From the beginning our favorites were the personable Cockatiels which quickly adapt to life in captivity and excell as household pets. Eventually we moved west to Perth and purchased a house in the country where we were able to construct several large outdoor aviaries, thus affording an opportunity to study the breeding biology and behavior of Cockatiels at close range.

In sharp contrast to many parts of our world today where wildlife seems to become more scarce with each passing moment, Australia offers, in our opinion, an almost unexcelled opportunity for the average person to observe a huge variety of unique plants and animals in their native surroundings. This is especially true with regards to the parrot fauna. Even as I write these words there is a pair of wild Red-Capped Parrots (*Purpuricephalus spurius*) perched just outside the window on a tall eucalypt. Three miles up the road there is a secluded wooded valley which harbors several pairs of Western Rosellas (*Platycercus icterotis*) and during the fall large flocks of White-Tail Black Cockatoos roost in the trees around our house. All of these are considered to be rare by world standards, but are locally common within the relatively tiny enclave which comprises the southwestern corner of Australia. On our trips to the north we have frequently seen huge flocks of wild Budgerigars, their bright green bodies flashing in the sunlight, as the flight path of the aggregation twists and turns. We have also seen an abundance of Cockatiels and there is no greater thrill for a parrot enthusiast than to see these magnificent birds on the wing in their native surroundings.

Shortly after we became seriously interested in maintaining and breeding Cockatiels we attempted to purchase an authoritative handbook on the subject, but were disappointed to find nothing of significance available. Therefore it is our desire to fill this gap with the preparation of the book. We admit to being relative newcomers to the avicultural hobby and are still learning previously unknown facets of the biology of these fascinating animals. Nevertheless, we feel that we have now accumulated enough worthwhile information to justify its publication.

We emphasize that the methodolgy described herein should not be considered as the *only* formula for achieving successful maintenance and breeding. For example there are a myriad of good aviary designs, and professional aviculturists have different opinions about diets and the rearing and taming of young birds. We acknowledge that there are many different and equally successful approaches to the art of Cockatiel keeping.

Gerald R. and Connie J. Allen
Perth, Australia

Harry Lacey is undoubtedly the world's leading bird photographer, and to show his excellent work. . .and to show a non-Australian parrot. . .these Yellow-Bellied Senegal Parrots, bred in England, are a typical example. The species is *Poicephalus s. senegalus*.

CHAPTER ONE

SELECTION AND PURCHASE

Cockatiels make ideal pets and rate second only to the Budgerigar in popularity among the many parrot-like species. There are thousands of Cockatiels owners in South Africa, America, Europe, and Australia. Few would trade their pets and most agree that for the comparatively low price there is no finer parrot-like bird to be found. It is difficult to single out the Cockatiel's most outstanding attribute. Some would say it is their relatively small size and attractive appearance. Others claim it is their hardiness and cleanliness. Still others extoll their intelligence and willingness to breed in captivity. To us it is a combination of all these factors that make Cockatiels so highly desirable, both as aviary birds and pets.

Cockatiels are generally available from the larger pet shops and many small ones. However, the demand is sometimes greater than the supply and it may be necessary to have your name placed on a waiting list. Although extremely numerous in the wilds of Australia there is a total export ban and therefore all birds sold in other parts of the world are the progeny of local domestic aviary stock.

Fortunately Cockatiels are exceptionally hardy birds and nearly all of those which are available for sale will be in good condition. However, there are a few things to be on the lookout for. When making your selection it is best to spend some time, 15-20 minutes at least, watching the behavior of the birds. Avoid buying any which show a general lethargy. especially those which remain motionless on the perch for extended periods with feathers fluffed and watery eyes. These are signs of illness. You should choose a Cockatiel which has a sleek outward appearance, and one which is relatively active and exhibits an interest in its feed. Contrary to the opinion of some people, they need not be purchased in pairs. Solitary birds will thrive in captivity and in some respects make better pets.

If the Cockatiel is intended as a pet you should make sure that it is a young one as they are the most readily tamed. If breeding stock is desired, and you want immediate results, then the birds should be about 1½ to two years of age. In most cases the pet dealer should be able to help with the determination of age and sex. Young birds are fairly easy to detect on the basis of their light grey bills compared with the dark grey bill of adults. Initially the bill is quite pinkish, but generally by an age of about two to three months it has taken on a greyish hue. In addition, young birds frequently have undeveloped feathers or "quills" on the top of the head, just behind the crest. General size is also helpful in detecting youngsters, particularly if there are adult birds present for comparison. Although about the same length as adults, the young are notably more slender and do not reach full size until about nine months of age or shortly after the first moult. Both male and female babies exhibit the same coloration which is essentially the same as that of adult females. They lack the bright yellow head of the adult male and possess yellow and grey bars on the underside of the body and on the tail feathers, and also large spots on the primary wing feathers. In our young birds we have noticed that the pale striping on the breast region is more prominent and extensive than on adult females. In addition, the crest is often more sparse than that of adults and is held erect most of the time (in adults the crest is frequently depressed, at least partially).

If both male and female babies look alike your next question will probably be "How do you tell them apart?" For very young Cockatiels up to five or six months of age this is not always an easy task. From our experience we can sometimes gauge the sex of each member of a particular brood by comparing coloration and voice. The birds with a larger proportion of yellow on the face, particularly on the throat, and those which are most vociferous will very often turn out to be the males. However, we have sometimes been wrong. Thus it can be difficult to determine sex when the birds are very young particularly if only one or two Cockatiels are involved

Baby Cockatiels are the easiest to tame when they are young. This is a perfect specimen for taming, since it's only four weeks old. (Below) A typical female Cockatiel. Photos by Dr. Gerald R. Allen.

Large flocks of Rose-Breasted Cockatoos are a common sight in Australia. These were photographed at Beverley Springs in the far north of Western Australia. (Below) These Red-Tailed Black Cockatoos were photographed in the wilds of the Kimberley Region of Western Australia. Cockatoos and cockatiels like dead trees.

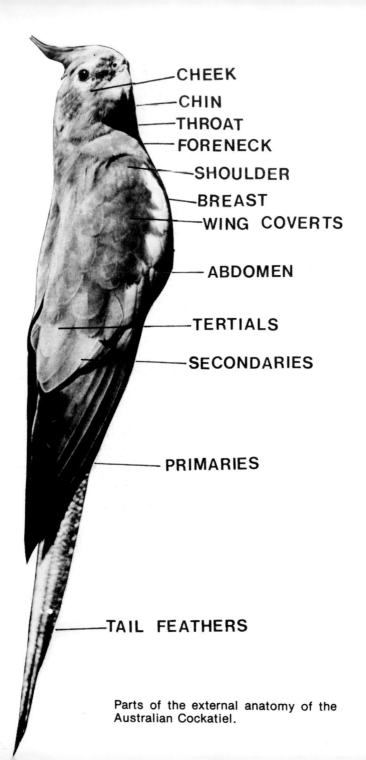

CHEEK

CHIN

THROAT

FORENECK

SHOULDER

BREAST

WING COVERTS

ABDOMEN

TERTIALS

SECONDARIES

PRIMARIES

TAIL FEATHERS

Parts of the external anatomy of the
Australian Cockatiel.

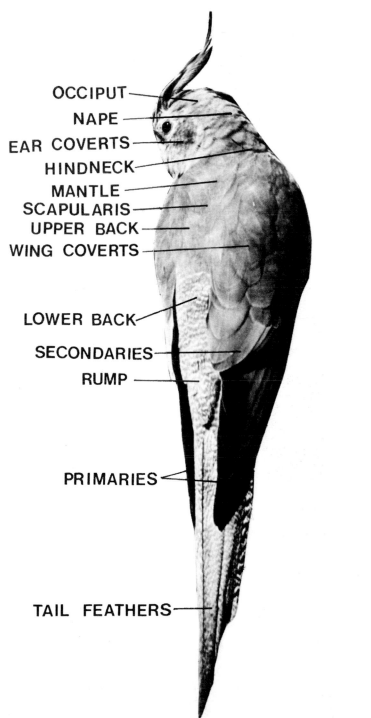

OCCIPUT

NAPE

EAR COVERTS

HINDNECK

MANTLE

SCAPULARIS

UPPER BACK

WING COVERTS

LOWER BACK

SECONDARIES

RUMP

PRIMARIES

TAIL FEATHERS

Cockatiels, like almost all other psittacines, keep themselves groomed and clean. They first use the gland at the base of their tail (photo lower right) to get the oil with which they groom themselves.

Tony and Mark Allen with their Cockatiel pets. The kids love the birds. . .and the birds love the kids.

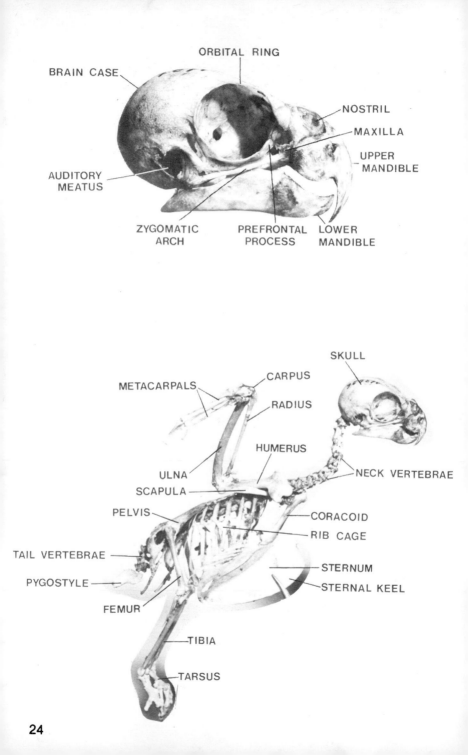

BRAIN CASE

ORBITAL RING

NOSTRIL

MAXILLA

UPPER
MANDIBLE

AUDITORY
MEATUS

ZYGOMATIC
ARCH

PREFRONTAL
PROCESS

LOWER
MANDIBLE

SKULL

METACARPALS

CARPUS

RADIUS

HUMERUS

NECK VERTEBRAE

ULNA

SCAPULA

PELVIS

CORACOID

RIB CAGE

TAIL VERTEBRAE

PYGOSTYLE

STERNUM

STERNAL KEEL

FEMUR

TIBIA

TARSUS

24

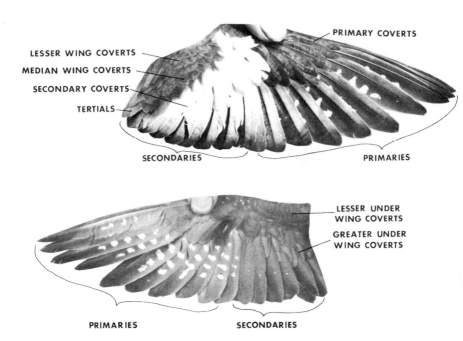

PRIMARY COVERTS

LESSER WING COVERTS

MEDIAN WING COVERTS

SECONDARY COVERTS

TERTIALS

SECONDARIES

PRIMARIES

LESSER UNDER WING COVERTS

GREATER UNDER WING COVERTS

PRIMARIES

SECONDARIES

The author, Dr. Gerald R. Allen, is a trained zoologist working on fishes. He has, for the first time, presented a Cockatiel's skull (upper photo, facing page) with the name of the main parts; the complete skeleton (bottom facing page); and the wing feathers with their correct nomenclature. Pay particular attention to the names of the feathers when you plan on clipping the wings. Photos by Gerald R. Allen.

Dr. and Mrs. Gerald R. Allen hand-raised these four-week-old Cockatiels. They have yet to take their first flight, but they are already
tame. Photo by Dr. Allen.

It is easy to recognize this as a young Cockatiel on the basis of the pale beak, incomplete crown feathering and extensive pronounced barring on the breast. Photo by Dr. Gerald R. Allen.

without the chance of comparison with others. Generally by the age of six to eight months, after the first moult takes place, males will begin to show their typical bright yellow facial coloration although we have encountered occasional males which had female feathering up until 1½ years of age. Some pet shops will guarantee male-female pairs, and if it turns out that both birds are the same sex they will exchange later on provided the bird is in good condition. However, such arrangements should be settled *at the time of purchase* to avoid bitter feelings later on. Both males and females make equally fine pets and can be easily tamed and trained to talk.

It is difficult to determine the age of adult birds and it is usually necessary to rely on the dealer for this information. However, bright colored males sometimes still have one or more of the barred tail feathers characteristic of juveniles. In this case you can determine that the age is probably somewhere between 14-18 months.

Nomenclature of the head and body external anatomy.

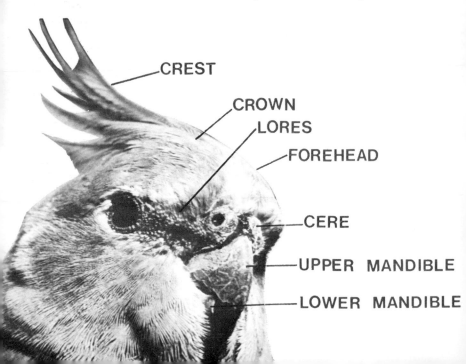

CREST

CROWN
LORES
FOREHEAD

CERE

UPPER MANDIBLE

LOWER MANDIBLE

CHAPTER TWO

CAGES

Cages come in a large variety of sizes and shapes. Unfortunately many are designed as decorator items for the household with very little thought for the eventual occupants. Cockatiels are creatures of wide open spaces and are powerful fliers. They should be provided with a roomy cage, preferably the size recommended for larger parrots. Smaller cages can be utilized, for example the larger budgie cages, but the birds should be released daily for exercise flights around the room. Canary breeding cages and budgie show cages are definitely not recommended. In these cramped quarters the tail feathers will be damaged quickly and the bird will lose condition.

Cages with only vertical wires should also be avoided as they make it difficult, if not impossible, for the Cockatiel to climb up the sides, which is one of their favorite pastimes. Also with this type of cage there is a danger of the head being thrust through the wires and the bird hanging itself for lack of a proper foothold. The cage construction should always include a series of vertical wires which will serve as sort of a ladder to facilitate climbing activities.

We prefer square cages which measure approximately 24 inches on each side. Many cages are equipped with sliding-tray floors which greatly facilitate cleaning. It is also desirable to line the sides with fine wire screen or a similar barrier for a distance of several inches above the bottom to avoid the messy scattering of seed on nearby floors and furniture.

The floor of the cage should be lined with paper. Commercial liners are available. Fine gravel or sand can be sprinkled over the paper and will help absorb droppings. In addition, a dish of feeding grit should be placed on the floor for reasons explained below.

The selection of cages for parrot-like birds is great. It is very important that the cage you select have both vertical and horizontal bars like those shown above. The cage should also have a wooden perch unless you have a special reason for not having a perch in the cage. Photo by the author.

Catching a wild, untamed Cockatiel is almost impossible without a bird net. First wait until the bird alights, then net him. . .but cover the top of the net with your hand or the Cockatiel will escape again. Photos by Brian Seed.

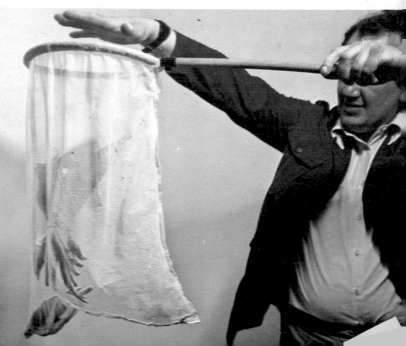

Be sure you buy your first Cockatiel cage from a pet shop so that the expert there can advise you about the good points and bad points of the particular cages available. Photos courtesy of Crown Cages and Prevue Metal Products. **Facing page:** If the horizontal wires of the cage are too far apart for your birds, you can use screening as a temporary covering to enable the birds to perch and climb up the sides of the cage. Photo by Manolo Guevara.

The cage should be cleaned regularly when it is convenient. Daily maintenance is not really necessary as Cockatiels are relatively clean animals. We find that twice weekly cleanings are perfectly adequate. This only takes a few minutes and basically consists of discarding the papers on the floor of the cage and replacing them with a fresh supply. A thorough cleaning is recommended about once a month or if mites are detected. This can be accomplished by immersing the cage in the bathtub or large basin of water and scrubbing it thoroughly with a stiff brush. A household germicide can be added to the wash water.

A good perch of natural, unfinished wood should be provided. If the cage is relatively small, one is adequate; for larger parrot cages, two or three can be utilized. However, it is important not to clutter the limited space with perches. Never use perches which have been painted as they may prove toxic. Those made of commerical doweling are readily available and attractive. Small, dead tree branches can also be utilized for this purpose. The exact diameter of the perch is not critical, but it should be roughly similar to an adult person's finger. Commercial cages are generally equipped with adequate water and seed containers. If not there are several different types for sale. Baked clay containers made of the same material as flower pots are available in assorted sizes and are adequate for both seeds and water. They should be placed on the floor of the cage, well away from the favorite perching spots to avoid fouling from the bird's droppings.

Cockatiels are curious animals and seem to enjoy "playing" with various objects suspended from the top or sides of the cage. There are a variety of bird toys available, many which include bells or a small mirror are especially appealing to Budgies and Cockatiels. Just remember this: as with perches, the cage should not be cluttered with lots of unsightly paraphernalia. One or two small items will do.

Birds which are allowed extended liberty periods can be provided with a "play-stand." These are generally constructed of dowel-rod and plywood and can be purchased commercially. Normally they include ladders and various perches, fixed or swinging, with mirrors, bells, or other toys attached.

A proper location for the Cockatiel's cage is important for your pet's well being. It should be placed in pleasant surroundings which are well ventilated, but not drafty, in short, a room which the owner would feel comfortable in if forced to spend prolonged periods there. Permanent window locations should be avoided, because of the harmful effect of possible drafts and prolonged exposure to sunlight, especially during the summer. Captive birds which are kept indoors generally have a thinner coat of insulating down and are very susceptible to drafts which may sometimes cause severe colds or even death.

As long as drafts are avoided Cockatiels can withstand relatively low overnight temperatures. It is not really necessary to keep the thermostat continually at 75°F. to insure their comfort. Overnight temperatures in the 50's and high 40's are easily tolerated, but the room should be warmed during the day to levels normally comfortable to humans (65° - 80°F.) In the wild, Cockatiels are found in areas where night temperatures go as low as 40 - 50°F. and daytime shade readings may exceed 110°F.

During warm months it is beneficial to take your Cockatiel outdoors for several hours each day whenever possible. The cage can be suspended from a tree branch or clothes-line which is located in the shade or in partial sunlight. If there is no threat of dogs, cats, or other animals the cage can be set on the grass and a makeshift sun shield should be provided with a towel or similar item laid across the cage top.

Great caution is necessary in putting birds with unclipped wings outside. Make sure the cage doors are latched and the floor is securely fastened. While living in Sydney we suspended a Cockatiel cage from the clothes-line one morning. One of our sons, who was seven at the time came running across the yard and accidentally collided with the cage completely knocking the separate floor section loose. In an instant two of our precious unclipped pets were airborne and disappeared over the hedge in full flight. We searched the vicinity for hours, but never found a trace of the pair.

It is best to shield your pets from loud disturbances, especially at night, when they would normally be sleeping. If you are planning a party or big get-together with lots of

These containers, made of baked clay, are economical and are well suited for both food and water. (Below) A female feeding from a commercial seed cup made of galvanized steel.

The proper position for clipping the Cockatiel's wing. In this case several of the secondaries and all the primaries are being cut from only one wing. (Below) Once the bird learns it cannot fly, it becomes much easier to tame.

small children running loose, we recommend placing the cage in an isolated room where the disturbance is mimimal. Smoke filled rooms are especially harmful and should be avoided. If for some reason it is not possible to darken the room containing your Cockatiel, shortly after nightfall the cage can be covered with a dark cloth. This will minimize disturbances and will insure the necessary rest.

CHAPTER THREE

FEEDING

Feeding is never a problem with healthy Cockatiels. A relatively simple diet consisting of a commercial parakeet or budgie mixture supplemented daily with fresh green food will provide most of the basic nutrients. We also feed our birds small unsalted sunflower seeds and occasionally small portions of mixed parrot or cockatoo seed which is available from pet and feed stores. Some owners recommend whole wheat bread crumbs, but we have tried this food without success. The birds simply refuse to eat it in most cases.

If you mix your own seed a satisfactory mixture consists of equal parts of canary seed and millet with smaller quantities of sunflower seeds and hulled oats. It is best not to buy large quantities of seed at one time, particularly in areas of high humidity. We generally purchase about a three to four week supply at a time. The seed should be stored in moisture proof containers, particularly if stored in a garage or outdoor feed shed. There are many different attractive cannisters made of glass or plastic on the market which make ideal seed containers.

Green foods are very important for their vitamin content and are essential for maintaining top condition. In many cases you will find an abundance of high quality green food growing right in your own yard, especially if you live in the country. When available, wild seeding grasses should be offered in generous portions. These can simply be placed on the floor of the cage and renewed daily. Weeds such as dandelions, plantain, foxtail, chickweed, milk thistles, and ripened grousel are all readily accepted. They especially relish the tiny seeds of lawn grass and the various wild varieties, sometimes spending hours picking on them and chewing the juicy stems. When seeding grasses and other wild green food are not available or if you live in a city without access to this sort of food, you can substitute by feeding such items as fresh spinach, watercress, fresh or frozen (thawed) green peas, carrot tops, celery, lettuce, and green corn. All of these items, of course, are available at your local grocery. Always offer the greens when fresh and remove the wilted uneaten portions from the cage on a daily basis. All green foods should be adequately washed with clean freshwater. Never offer foods which are likely to be contaminated.

Cockatiels are not particularly fond of fruit, but some will accept an occasional bit of apple. Your pets should not be offered table scraps such as mashed potatoes, cooked meats, seasoned salads, etc. Although they may eat these items there is a good chance they will cause digestive problems.

There are various color conditioners, breeding foods, vitamins, and other tonics available, but we have found these to be totally unnecessary if Cockatiels are supplied with the essential natural foods outlined above.

CHAPTER FOUR

GRIT AND CUTTLEBONE

We cannot overemphasize the importance of grit and cuttlebone for the well being of your pet. Grit is essential for the proper utilization of most dietary items, particularly seeds. The grit is ingested and stored in small quantities in the gizzard. The thick muscular walls of this organ expand

Cuttlebone is an
essential ingredient
in the diet of captive
Cockatiels.

The nest log is about
three feet long and
has an opening of five
inches.

The basic seed mixture for Cockatiels is the same as that used for Budgerigars (left), but can be supplemented with sunflower seeds (right) and mixed parrot seed (upper).

Cockatiels are frequently encountered in the vicinity of small streams and water holes such as this one at Beverley Springs, Australia.

and contract when food is eaten and this action, in combination with the grit particles, serves to grind the food up so it can be readily digested. The grit also provides minerals and necessary trace elements, as does cuttlebone. The latter is also a source of calcium which is vital for maintaining a healthy and strong beak. Cuttlebone is extremely important at breeding time and contributes to the development of strong, normal eggshells and is instrumental in preventing egg-binding. Brooding parents will spend long periods chewing on cuttlebone. In fact their normal consumption is more than doubled or tripled at this time.

Prepared bird grit is available at any pet shop and most supermarkets. You can also make your own. We use the following recipe:

> two lbs. clean, dry sand
> two lbs. assorted beach shells (finely crushed)
> ¼ lb. crushed charcoal
> ½ lb. of pulverized soft red brick
> 6 large pulverized cuttlebones

This amount generally lasts for over a year for about ten cockatiels. You should use a separate grit container (a small one of red baked clay is ideal) placed on the floor in a corner of the cage. Fill up the container occasionally and completely change the grit about once every two months. Chunks of insecticide-free soil or sod are also good sources of natural grit. When feeding seed grasses it is sometimes possible to pull them up by the roots with pieces of soil attached.

Cuttlebones are readily available from pet stores at a nominal price. We live close to the seashore and are able to obtain a year's supply free of charge by walking several miles along the beach. Cuttlebone hunting is best right after periods of rough seas as many are cast high up on the shore. Commercial cuttlebones sometimes have a clip for attachment to the cage. If not you can poke two small holes through the middle of the bone with an icepick or nail and then run a fine gauge wire through the holes for attachment to the side of the cage, preferably in a position in which it can be reached from the perch.

CHAPTER FIVE

BATHING

Many Cockatiels enjoy frequent baths, particularly during hot weather. On several occasions we have seen wild Cockatiels bathing on the edges of small pools in a nearly dry streambed.In nature the birds are also "bathed" regularly during rain showers. However, some captive Cockatiels are not overly fond of water and should not be forced to bathe. Even without water they are capable of keeping perfectly clean by means of their meticulous grooming activity. During preening the bird periodically obtains a bit of oil from a special gland located near the base of the tail. It will appear as though the Cockatiel is biting its vent region. After the oil is transferred to the surface of the beak it is then rubbed over the feathers.

We use red baked clay dishes for our bird baths, but any shallow bowl which is reasonably heavy (so it cannot be easily tipped over) will do. If the cage is relatively small it is not necessary to leave the bathing dish in at all times. It can be placed in the cage for approximately 30 minutes every few days (more frequently during warm weather). Generally Cockatiels are not messy bathers and will not do much splashing. The normal habit is to simply wade into the bath and wet only the legs and feathers covering the belly. If your Cockatiels are fond of water they can also be bathed outside of the cage, either in a dish or even in the kitchen sink. Many owners who allow their pets to roam freely about the house report that Cockatiels will frequently fly to the sink as soon as they hear the sound of running water.

The bath water for Cockatiels should not be overly hot or too cold. Water which is about human body temperature (i.e., lukewarm) is just about right, although cooler water is appreciated on hot summer days. If the birds are placed outside during warm weather they can be sprayed for a minute with a fine mist from the garden hose. Some owners also give indoor showers from a window-spray cleaner bottle or simil-

This feeding tray has a low guard rail to prevent the inevitable spillage which results from Cockatiel feeding. (Below) Aviary Cockatiels love sunflower seeds.

A brightly colored male Cockatiel chews on cuttlebone after feeding on seed. (Below) You may use a single dish for drinking water and bathing, but the water must be changed daily.

ar sort of atomizer. Just remember only a few light squirts are necessary. Do not thoroughly douse the bird.

Cockatiels usually preen or groom themselves for several minutes after bathing. This is to set the feathers back in place which have been disarranged during the bathing process. If you are a new Cockatiel owner you will be surprised with its fastidiousness in keeping every feather in place.

One last bit of advice with regards to bathing. . .*only use clear freshwater* for this purpose. Never add any type of soaps, bath oils, or pet shampoos.

CHAPTER SIX

TAMING

We know of no bird which is easier to tame than the Cockatiel. However, if the bird is to be tamed for a pet it is important to have a young one, preferably less than 12-14 weeks of age. Older birds can be gradually tamed, but it takes a great deal of time and patience and they are usually never as friendly as birds tamed at a young age.

We have used two basic methods to tame baby Cockatiels. The first of these consists of hand feeding them from an early age as described in Chapter Twelve. If you have bred chicks in your own home and wish to hand rear them for pets they can be taken from the parents after the eyes are open at an age ranging between one to two weeks. If the parents are very tame and not bothered by your presence around the chicks, the young need not be permanently removed from the nest, but can be removed for brief periods of handling which will result in tame birds by the time they are weaned.

Personally we think that hand rearing is an unnecessary waste of much time and worrying. We only use this method if the parents, for some reason, are not able to rear the babies themselves. If you have a nest of chicks it is best to let nature take its course and not attempt to tame the birds until after they have left the nest and are at the weaning stage, which brings us to the second method of taming.

If your chicks have just been weaned by their natural parents or you have obtained a young bird from a pet shop, taming is a very simple exercise and most of the work can be accomplished in less than an hour! Our most recent taming session took place two evenings ago and it took a mere 20 minutes before the Cockatiel was finger tame and sitting comfortably on a shoulder perch. Some authorities claim that it is best to wait a week or more after first bringing the Cockatiel into its new home before attempting to train it. It is claimed that taming is much easier after the bird is familiar with the sights and sounds of its new surroundings. Again, we have found this to be a pure waste of time. On the contrary, we find that no acclimation is necessary! The bird should be tamed as soon as possible, even during the first hour in the new home.

To begin taming, first place the cage in a relatively small, quiet room. An ideal situation is one with very little furniture which greatly facilitates retrieving the bird during the first few moments of liberty. Next slowly place your hand in the cage and firmly grasp (but not too tight) the bird around the wings. Chances are it will bite your hand, but at this age it is impossible to inflict real damage, other than a painful nip. It is important not to release the bird or quickly jerk back your hand when it attempts to bite. This will only encourage the bird to continue this behavior and will make taming difficult. Just let it bite you and in a few seconds it will release its grip. Once it knows that the bite has not deterred you, chances are it will not bite again. We have experienced many birds which never bite during the taming process.

After removing the Cockatiel from its cage the next step is to clip one of the wings, which will greatly aid you in controlling the bird during this initial session. The process is painless and will not detract from the overall appearance of your pet if done properly. Clipped wings will completely regenerate within six months. However, it is a good idea to re-

Although Cockatiels are being bred in a number of color varieties, the number of color varieties of Cockatiel is much smaller than the number of different color varieties of Budgerigar. Photo by Manolo Guevara at Paterson Bird Store.

clip after they grow back, especially if the birds are allowed to roam at liberty around the house. If only one wing is clipped they still possess limited flight capabilities, yet can be retrieved in the event they should accidentally escape through an open door or window. Various methods of wing clipping are described in Chapter Seven.

It is best for only one person to do the initial taming, although a helper is sometimes needed for the wing clipping, which only takes a few seconds. If there are one or more onlookers, make sure they remain quiet and relatively motionless on the sidelines. During your first contacts with the bird it is important to move slowly and steadily without sudden jerks, especially of the arms and hands. Also it is a good idea to talk and whistle softly to your pet throughout the taming session so it will become accustomed to your voice.

It is advisable not to attempt taming more than one Cockatiel at a time. If you have a pair to tame keep them isolated from one another during the initial session and if possible for the next several days. If they are allowed together their interest will be greatly diverted and taming becomes difficult. For this reason solitary birds frequently make the best pets.

After the wing has been clipped gently release the Cockatiel about one foot above the floor. Usually it will try to fly in short bursts around the room, but soon learns that it cannot gain much altitude, nor fly in a straight line. Generally it will then scamper about the floor, sometimes huddling in a corner or behind a piece of furniture. At this stage you should slowly approach the bird and surround it from below with your outstretched fingers. With a little coaxing it will hop onto your hand. Let the Cockatiel perch comfortably there and then slowly lift your hand off the floor until you are in a standing position. During the lifting process the bird may once again fly to the floor. If this happens start over again. After several trials it will be content to remain seated on the top of your hand. At this stage you can begin stroking it gently on the breast with one finger.

When the bird is used to this movement after a minute or two offer your finger as a perch at a level slightly above that of your other hand. The Cockatiel can be coaxed to climb up onto the finger by pressing the side of the finger into the breast region, thus throwing the bird off balance. It will instinctively climb onto your finger for a better foothold. Keep repeating this procedure until the bird climbs up from one finger to another. Now you can try gently scratching the sides and top of the head, but don't persist if the bird objects. Some Cockatiels simply do not like to have their heads scratched no matter how tame they may happen to be.

After these first basic steps it is only a matter of the bird getting used to you. If it insists on repeatedly flying on to the floor, be persistent in retrieving it, but always in a gentle manner. The Cockatiel will very quickly learn that you intend it no harm. About midway through the taming session, once the bird has learned to remain perched on your finger or hand for several minutes at a time, you can teach it to sit on your shoulder. With the pet securely perched on your finger slowly bring it to a position next to the shoulder. Then roll the finger away with a twisting motion so the Cockatiel will be forced to climb aboard your shoulder to gain a more secure foothold. For the remainder of the session you can allow the bird to sit there. After a minute or two it may fly to the floor but after a few futile attempts will learn to remain in place.

After the first taming session you can handle your pet for gradually longer intervals each day. They are very responsive to the attentions of a devoted owner and will quickly learn to spend long periods riding about on your shoulder or the top of your head. However, if you decide to encourage this practice an old shirt or blouse is recommended as *we have not yet encountered a housebroken Cockatiel.*

Older juveniles and young adults can be tamed using this same method, but it generally takes longer as they are more easily frightened and hence more difficult to calm down. The bite of these older birds can be quite painful and may draw blood. Therefore we recommend the wearing of tight fitting leather gloves. You can gain similar protection by wrapping the index and middle fingers with several layers of masking or adhesive tape. If there is doubt about the age

Cockatiel embryo.

Nine days old.

Four days old.

Six days (left) and nine days (right).

Six days old.

Ten days old.

Seven days old.

Twelve days old.

Thirteen days old.

Nineteen days old.

Fourteen days old.

A family portrait: 21, 19 and 17 days old from left to right.

Fifteen days old.

Twenty days old.

Seventeen days old.

Twenty-two days old.

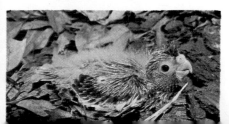

of the bird or if it seems to have a particularly nasty tempera-
ment (hissing is a good indication) it is better to be cautious
by wearing gloves or tape. When they bite, the mandibles
are rotated from side to side in a very painful and prolonged
nip. The bird can be forced to release its hold by lightly
thumping it under the chin. Birds which bite should never be
flicked on the beak or immersed in water as punishment as
this will frequently contribute to a bad disposition, which
may be difficult to overcome.

CHAPTER SEVEN

WING CLIPPING

Wing clipping is quick and easy and is good insurance
against the possible tragic escape of your pet. No matter how
tame, unclipped Cockatiels should not be allowed even a
moment of freedom, for the chances are great that your pet
will take to the air and you will never see it again. Moreover,
clipping the wings greatly facilitates the taming process as
explained in Chapter Six.

For quick clips with untamed Cockatiels it is best to em-
ploy two persons, one to hold the bird securely and position
the wing, and the other to do the actual clipping. The bird
should be held firmly, but gently in the manner illustrated in

the accompanying photographs. With one hand the holder extends one wing which can be clipped in several ways. The quickest and preferred method of clipping young birds for taming is to simply cut all the primaries from one side. This still allows limited flight with the opposite wing, which is important for exercise, and does not greatly detract from the overall appearance. Another type of clip which some owners perfer is to cut several of the secondaries and all of the primaries except the outer two or three. This clip is done on one or both wings and preserves the long, graceful appearance of the flight feathers when the wings are folded. It also allows limited flight. There are a variety of other clips in use which depend on personal taste, but all give basically the same result.

Our clipping tool consists of a pair of sharp barber scissors. Generally we start the clip from the middle of the wing and cut outwards at the level of the primary coverts. Do not go under the coverts, especially on birds that are moulting, as the base of new feathers contain tiny blood vessels which can be severed, causing pain and bleeding. If by accident you should cut one of these, the pain is very brief and bleeding stops very quickly due to the strong coagulating properties of bird blood.

55

A beautiful male Cockatiel among the eucalypt foliage in the authors' natural aviary.

Thirty days old and ready for taming!

CHAPTER EIGHT

TEACHING YOUR COCKATIEL TO TALK

Parrots and parrot-like birds are renowned for their ability to repeat words and phrases, recite poetry, and whistle tunes. Cockatiels are not really the best talkers in the family, but nevertheless can be taught if a certain amount of patience on the part of the owner is exercised. Solitary pets make the best talkers. Indeed, it is usually impossible to teach pairs to talk, at least if they are always kept together. They are simply more interested in each other than the distractive teaching attempts of the owner.

Repetition is the key to teaching your Cockatiel to talk. The words should be relatively simple (*"hello"* is a good starter) and repeated clearly over and over, from a short distance away. Generally speaking, most parrots will respond more quickly to high pitched voices such as those of women or children. If you have neither the time nor the patience for numerous training sessions there are records available from pet shops expressly designed to teach your pets various words and phrases. A tape recorder can also be utilized for this purpose. There is no way to predict how long it will take to achieve results. Some birds respond within a week, others take over a year. Repetition and patience on the part of the owner are valuable virtues in this undertaking. Some owners insist on offering rewards, such as special seed treats, after the desired words are repeated.

When teaching your Cockatiel to talk it is advisable to adhere to a uniform schedule of daily training sessions. One half hour each day is sufficient for this purpose. Once your pet says the desired word or phrase it should be prompted to repeat it over and over until the pronunciation is clear. After a few days a new word or phrase can be introduced, but don't make things too complicated. The first word is usually the most difficult, but once spoken, others are learned readily.

CHAPTER NINE

HOUSEHOLD BREEDING

After you have successfully tamed your Cockatiel and have kept it as a pet for a period of time chances are you will become even more enthusiastic about these magnificent animals. To advance your hobby, the next logical step is to obtain a mate of the opposite sex. Once this is accomplished the desire to breed them and raise a nest of babies usually becomes overwhelming. Cockatiels are an excellent choice for the budding aviculturist as they are one of the easiest parrot-like birds to breed in captivity. However, there are a few basic rules which should be followed, otherwise your attempts will prove to be futile.

It is much easier to breed your Cockatiel in an outside aviary built around a tree than inside your home, but it is done every day in all parts of the world.

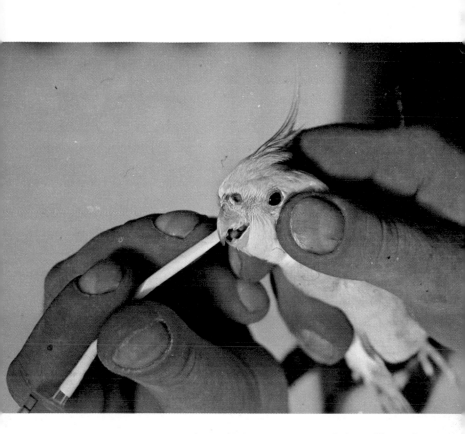

The proper way to hold a Cockatiel to give it medicine. Photo by Manolo Guevara.

Opposite:
A nicely colored new Cockatiel strain. Photo by Brian Seed.

Captive Cockatiels can be brought into breeding condition any time of the year with proper temperature control and a correct diet. Normal household temperatures comfortable to humans will prove adequate. It is especially important to feed a good supply of green foods both prior to nesting and while it is in progress. Feedings of seeding grasses are desirable during the nesting period and for this reason we recommend that the first breeding attempt take place in the spring or early summer when there is an abundance of wild food. An ample supply of grit mixture (not just sand or gravel) and cuttlebone are also important for successful breeding.

Cockatiels which are constantly confined to a household cage, even a fairly large one, will rarely breed. Therefore it is necessary to allow the birds extended liberty periods. If you can give them a small room of their own and leave the cage door constantly open this is the ideal situation. It is sometimes possible to do this in a room which is seldom used such as a guest room, basement (heated if necessary), etc.

We have never bred Cockatiels indoors because we have such ideal conditions for outdoor aviary breeding in Australia. Therefore our knowledge in this area is very limited. However an excellent account of household breeding has been written by Nancy Curtis (*Cockatiels*, T.F.H.) and in the remaining pages of this chapter we quote from Chapter Nine of her publication:

The first step is to get them into excellent condition for breeding. This means enriching their diet with foods not normally supplied, and you will note that these foods are all mineral enriched. I have found the following mixture to be the most beneficial in getting birds in breeding condition. This will last one pair about a week.

> ¼ cup Parakeet seed
> ½ cup commercial nesting food
> ⅓ cup oats
> ¼ cup condition food

Mix this together and feed in one container.

Add about four full drops of wheat germ oil over the

amount placed in the feeding dish. The regular amount of sunflower seeds should be fed separately in another dish.

Plenty of cuttlebone, calcium block, oyster shell and grit should be available, the latter two items in large quantities and changed daily. Lettuce and carrot should be fed daily to keep the bowels loose. If they appear constipated, a little lime water (2 or 3 drops) added to their drinking water will remedy this. A piece of whole wheat bread, soaked in water and dotted with wheat germ oil, will be an aid in breeding.

Birds raised in outside aviaries are inclined to breed in the spring and fall, but it is not uncommon to find them breeding all year round. Consequently, house birds, unaccustomed to radical temperature changes, may be bred at any time. There is less danger of egg binding when the birds are bred indoors in the winter. However, in the summer they are more subject to mites and this discomfort may cause them to break the eggs while scratching themselves. They may become too warm in the nest box and desert the eggs. The breeder must use his own judgment to prevent this if he plans to breed at this time.

The aforementioned diet is extremely rich and caution must be exercised to see that the birds do not get overly fat. There is but one remedy for this, and perhaps it is the most important of all: THE BIRDS SHOULD BE GIVEN ALL THE EXERCISE AND FLIGHT ROOM POSSIBLE. They must feel as free as though they were in their native woods. The cage door should be left open at all times. If you are fussy about your furniture, or are not around to clean up after them, better not try breeding in the house. They are messy, but only at this time, when chewing and activity is so important.

A nest box should be placed as near to the cage as possible, on top, or at least where, when they are flying, they can both view it. With their freedom, nest box, and the enriched diet, you will note that the copulation period is longer. At this time, a check should be made of the vents of both birds, to insure that there are no overgrown feathers that may interfere with the mating.

THE NEST BOX

The nest box should be wooden and have a partition in the middle to keep the eggs from rolling too much. It should be large; this is stressed for two reasons:

1. Both birds incubate the eggs and spend hours together in the box. They need room to move freely and turn the eggs.
2. The nest box will act as "nursery" for the chicks until they are old enough to leave it.

The box should have a 3½ inch hole in the center and a perch outside to make access easier. In fact, everything should be done to make the nest box convenient and easily accessible. The female is especially cautious at this time. There must be no fear of entering or leaving it. If the box is too small and they both try to get inside, they may step on the eggs or roll them together and break them. They can be patched, either with clear fingernail polish or a piece of another egg, but usually by the time the damage is discovered, part of the fluid has been lost and the egg is useless. IT IS IMPORTANT TO HAVE A LARGE NEST BOX, the ideal being at least 16" x 16". The partition should mark off about half this area.

As soon as the nest box is placed in the cage, both birds will investigate, and begin scratching and chewing on it. It is necessary for the breeder to help them with material to lay the eggs on. Shavings, Pablum or some other soft material (but never cotton or cloth) should be placed about 1 inch deep on the floor. They will arrange this to their liking.

Copulation between the male and female continues right up until the egg is laid. However, two or three days before the first egg is laid, the female exhibits obvious signs of pregnancy. There is a lump on the underside of her tail near the vent. Although the male continues with his lovemaking, and during the actual act of copulation will take longer, the female seems uninterested. Her tail feathers will become ragged from spending so much time in the box and arranging the material for the eggs. She often appears puffed up and she ruffles herself regularly. She assumes a more bloated and "hunched" position on the perch. Her breathing appears to rack her whole body.

During the entire nesting period she continues her normal pattern of bathing, often coming out of the nest box twice a day to bathe. The bath water should be at least room temperature as a guard against chilling and egg binding. She does this to keep the eggs moist.

On the days the eggs are laid, both birds will stay in the nest box together. At times one or the other will come out to eat. The female always visits the grit tray and calcium block. This procedure continues during the entire incubation period. Their schedule is so arranged that after all the eggs are laid, the male spends nearly all day on the eggs, and the female eats, bathes and enjoys flight and freedom. She will on occasion relieve him to eat and drink, and will sometimes sit with him, at which time they share the eggs. At night, however, the female sits and the male stands outside the box or locates himself very near the cage or nest box entrance.

A clutch of eggs varies from 4 to 8. The more eggs, the closer the female must be watched. With each egg she labors, sometimes the labor lasting as long as 10 hours. Her breathing becomes heavier, she appears more tired, and there will be a spasmodic twitching of the tail. At the actual time the egg is laid, she will back into a corner, her tail is propped on the side of the box and head nearly rests on the floor. Here she strains for up to an hour. As soon as the egg is laid, she rolls it with her beak to the center of the box. Then she tucks it gently under her breast and the incubation begins. During the egg-laying process, the male sits on the already laid eggs. He continues to stay with her until she is rested and capable of setting on the whole clutch. The turning of the eggs is done, as described above. This is mostly done by the female and it is with genuine loving and gentle care that she rolls and turns the eggs, then once again tucks them carefully under her breast.

It would be reasonably accurate to say that the eggs are laid about every 48 to 52 hours—that is, every other day. Unless it is absolutely necessary, it is not wise to disturb the nest. Despite the fact that removing the eggs as they are laid, and replacing them with plastic eggs—returning the full clutch when the egg laying period is finished—will contribute to hatching the babies all at the same time, rather than every other day as they should, this procedure will keep the hen on the nest for at least another week. She may get tired and desert the nest before the incubation period is completed.

When all the chicks hatch at once, this exerts a greater problem for feeding on the parents and they may neglect them completely. Instinct has a way of knowing when nature has been tampered with, and no matter how faithful to the eggs the mother is, these factors may contribute to her leaving the nest before the eggs have hatched, or before the chicks are capable of caring for themselves. Unless you have access to a commercial incubator, the eggs are best left strictly to the parents' care.

During the last days of incubation, the eggs to be hatched first will be left to one side for a period of time each day. This may be to allow the chick to cool inside the shell, thus preparing it for its hatching. Also during the latter part of the incubation period of those eggs that have not yet hatched, the male spends more time in the nest box and often cares for the chicks at night while the female sets on the remaining eggs.

On the 18 or 19th day after the egg has been laid, a tiny hole appears in the side of the egg. At this time the chick can be heard chipping at the shell and making his very first "chirps." Just a matter of hours later, the chick emerges from the shell. The parents clean the baby, for there is a kind of afterbirth encrusted on his body. Shortly thereafter they will feed the little one by regurgitating food into its mouth. It is best to leave the chicks with the parents for a few days. They do seem to get a better start by doing this.

A Cockatiel egg compared to a Chicken egg. Photo by Manolo Guevara.

At times the parents do not feed the chicks, and they must be hand fed. The main reason the parent birds do not feed the chicks is that they have not been provided with proper food. A mixture of equal parts of nesting food, Pablum and strained bananas should be moistened with water and placed in the cage a week before the eggs are to hatch. Again, add two drops of wheat germ oil to this mixture.

Should the chick be stuck in the shell due to insufficient moisture (again the importance of available bathing facilities for the parents) the pair will throw the egg from the nest. These discarded eggs should be removed. Once the birds begin eating and picking at the eggs, they can never be trusted again and may try to destroy other eggs, even though their original intention was to help free the chick. Once the eggs have been discarded or abused by the parents, there is little once can do to save the unborn chick. The egg may be rubbed with a moistened cloth and incubated with a light bulb, but the chances are slim that the egg will hatch.

During the entire incubation period, the parents keep the nest box spotlessly clean. They contain all their droppings within themselves until they are well away from the nest box. Because of this, it may be alarming to the novice breeder to note the size and color of the droppings, which are large, loose and a lighter shade of green. There is also a considerable amount of white, due to the excess intake of gravel and calcium. If the droppings are actually runny, the bowels can be tightened by lessening the amount of lettuce or lime water. However, at this time the bird should not become constipated and it is safer for the bowels to be a little loose.

Before beginning the breeding period, the birds should be examined closely for mites, and if during the incubation period they are suspected, the birds should be sprayed with a good mite spray. This can be done while they are outside the nest box (so as not to damage the eggs). A preventive measure can be taken by spraying the nest box when setting it up, as well as the cage. Both cage and nest box should be well cleaned before starting, for aside from cleaning the bottom of the nest after the babies are hatched, it is difficult to clean the cage while the parents are nesting.

CHAPTER TEN

AVIARY BREEDING

WHEN TO BREED

Over much of their natural range Cockatiels breed during the springtime. It is during this period, after the winter rains, that there is an abundance of seeding grasses which are vital for feeding the nestlings. It is therefore logical to breed captive Cockatiels during this same period. In cooler climates you should wait until late spring or early summer. In very moderate, temperate climates, such as those experienced in Southern California or southwestern Australia, breeding can take place at nearly any time of the year. The birds will not breed without a suitable nest and therefore the cycle is easily controlled. Quite simply put, if a nest site is not provided, there will be no breeding. Once the nest box or log is introduced breeding will ensue if the birds are in good health and of proper age.

In nature Cockatiels produce one nest per year and occasionally two nests if there is abundant rainfall and consequently plenty of food available. The estimated lifespan is 10-15 years; therefore, the total number of young which is produced by a pair during their lifetime could be estimated at approximately 175-200. This figure is based on an average brood size of five. In captivity, particularly in mild climates, it is not unusual to raise two broods per year and even more is possible although not recommended. The entire breeding cycle takes about 2½ months from the time the eggs are laid until the chicks are weaned. If possible the birds should be given a month or two rest period between successive broods, but sometimes new eggs will be laid shortly after the last brood is out of the nest and are still dependent on the parents for food. In this case the period is not possible.

To discourage breeding you can either block off the nest entrance or remove the nest completely. We do not recommend more than two broods per year as it is unnatural and will most likely lead to a run-down condition in your breeding stock, giving rise to infertile eggs or chicks which may not be properly cared for. For these reasons we generally remove the nest log from the aviary after the second brood is produced and do not replace it for several months.

No special efforts are really needed to bring the adults into breeding condition. Special commercial conditioning foods are completely unnecessary. As previously mentioned in Chapter Three, your Cockatiels should be provided with a balanced diet comprised of daily feedings of mixed parakeet seed, sunflower seed, green food, grit, and cuttlebone. These essentials should be provided the year round whether breeding is intended or not. Birds kept on a nutrient rich diet such as this will remain in so-called "breeding-condition" at all times. However, we do feel that it is advantageous to feed seeding grasses, either picked from lawns and gardens (or a vacant lot), or grown in the aviary as they very closely simulate the food which is eaten in the natural habitat.

THE NEST

The nest consists of either a hollow log or rectangular box. We prefer logs, because they are natural breeding sites for wild Cockatiels. However, these are sometimes difficult to obtain, particularly if you live in the city. Furthermore, they can prove to be troublesome if your aviaries are prone to mite infestations as the numerous cracks and fissures of a log will quickly be utilized as a home by these pests.

If you decide to use a log, one which is two or three feet in length and about eight to 15 inches in diameter will be suitable. The exact diameter of the hollow is not critical, but it should not be too small. One which is five to ten inches across is generally sufficient. The log should be positioned near the ceiling of the aviary and tilted at approximately a 45° angle. It should then be securely fastened. A position under the shelter is suitable, although anywhere in the flight is satisfactory. If outside of the shelter, the opening of the log should be placed away from the prevailing winds and it is advisable to fashion the log (by cutting if necessary) so there is a sort of hooded effect at the opening to shield against rain. However, a certain amount of rain which may enter the hol-

Cockatiel color mutations are becoming more common; this is a pair of unusual cinnamon Cockatiels. Photo by Brian Seed.

Opposite:
This is an adult pied (also called harlequin) hen; the fully symmetrical pattern is not produced very often. Photo by Brian Seed.

low will not prove harmful as the eggs and young chicks are adequately shielded by the nesting parents.

If the log has open cracks or sutures it may be necessary to plug these before installation. For this purpose we utilize regular wall plaster applied with a putty knife. The end of the log opposite the opening can be plugged by nailing or gluing on either a circular or square piece of plywood or metal. It is very important to provide a nest perch near the entrance of the log. This can be constructed by wiring or nailing a short section of tree branch or dowel-rod to the side of the nest log.

If a nest box is utilized rather than a log it should be rectangular in shape, approximately 12 x 16 inches, with a height of about 12 inches. A circular hole of three to four inches diameter leads into the nesting compartment and is located near the top of the box at the middle of one side. A short piece of dowel-rod should be provided for a perch just below the entrance hole. A hinged lid will facilitate cleaning and periodic inspections of the nest. The box should be placed in a high position in the aviary similar to that recommended for nest logs.

Wild Cockatiels do not require special nesting materials other than the nest hollow itself. Therefore it is not really necessary to provide your nest box or hollow log with extra frills in the false belief that you will be making the birds more comfortable. It is particularly harmful to add materials which will accumulate moisture, thus providing a breeding ground for molds and harmful bacteria. If a nest box is utilized it is advisable to scoop out (with a chisel) a shallow depression in one corner of the floor near the back wall. This will provide a place where the eggs can be safely deposited without fear of them rolling freely around the flat bottom. The same results can be achieved by gluing a pair of three or four inch sticks in one corner to form a low enclosure. Although we do not use extraneous nesting material some aviculturists advocate a layer of dry leaves, bark, wood shavings, Pablum, sawdust, or peat to prevent egg rolling and to help absorb the droppings of the baby birds.

If possible the nest box or log should be thoroughly

washed and disinfected after each brood is fledged. This is usually an easy matter with a nest box, but more difficult with a cumbersome log. At any rate the latter should be cleaned at least once per year preferably just prior to the onset of the breeding season.

COURTSHIP

During the courtship period the pair will stay incessantly together and there is much mutual preening and exploratory activity in the vicinity of the nest site. There are no elaborate behavioral displays as in many other birds. Instead the male frequently takes a position near the female, depresses the crest and lifts it's shoulders and holds the wings out from the body, but keeps the wing tips folded across the back at the same time. The head is held very high and the characteristic melodic Cockatiel call is repeated several times in succession. A.H. Lendon described another courtship display as follows: *"The display is rarely given, usually only when a female is first introduced to a male that has led a bachelor existence for some time. It consists of a series of rather absurd looking hops whilst following the female along the ground and is accompanied by a low warbling variant of the usual shrill call note."*

Although the male does not have a penis it mounts the female in mammal fashion during copulation. Its claws are used to gain a secure foothold on the females back. This is why lame males with damaged legs or feet are frequently useless for breeding. Individual copulatory periods generally last one or two minutes and several may occur in a single day. During copulation the female lifts the anterior section of the wings and emits a repetitive soft squeaking noise. The male shuffles its tail from side to side, periodically depressing it to bring the vent into contact with that of the female. During copulation the male is generally silent but repeatedly opens and closes its mandibles. This behavior has been termed "the bill clicking display" by J. Courtney and is a typical cockatoo characteristic. Sperm passes from the male's testes via the sperm duct to the cloaca, and then is transferred to the cloaca of the female. From this point sperm passes up the oviduct and meets the ovum and fertilization occurs. The egg then passes back down the oviduct where first the albumen or egg white is secreted and then the shell is formed in a sort of assembly line fashion. We are not certain of the gestation period for Cockatiels but it appears to be very brief, perhaps only a few days from copulation to egg laying.

INCUBATION

The average nest contains about five eggs, but the number may range from three to nine. The eggs are pure white and many times smaller than a small chicken egg. We measured several from a recent nest which averaged 20.3 mm x 26.6 mm or roughly ¾ inch x one inch. The eggs are laid at approximately two day intervals, which means that each egg and subsequent chick in the nest is at a different stage of development. Hence at the end of the nesting period all the chicks do not leave the nest at the same time, but rather over a period of several days.

Both the male and female take turns sitting on the eggs. The female usually sits throughout the night and is relieved at various times during the day by the male, allowing her a chance to feed, water, bathe, and chew on the cuttlebone. The parents sit very tightly, that is nearly continually, during the incubation stage. The eggs generally hatch about 21 days after they are laid, but this figure can vary from 18 to 23 days in some circumstances.

If for some reason the parents abandon the nest it may be possible to hatch the eggs (provided they are fertile, of course) with the use of a poultry incubator or heat lamp. However, this approach seldom succeeds as it is very difficult to simulate the natural temperature and humidity conditions. Therefore never remove eggs from the nest for artificial incubation unless you are absolutely certain they have been abandoned.

If the hatching is overdue and there is doubt about the fertility of the eggs they can easily be tested by holding the egg up in the sunlight or inspecting it by shining a strong light through it. If the egg is fertile and development of the embryo has proceeded for more than about four or five days, the numerous branching dark blood vessels will be readily apparent or you will be able to see the outline of the embryo itself if development has proceeded far enough. An infertile egg will be uniformly translucent without blood vessels or any hint of an embryo.

MUTATIONS AND HYBRIDS

Contrary to the situation with the Canary and Budgerigar, aviculturists have not succeeded in producing a multitude of color varieties in the Cockatiel. However, an occasional mutant is not uncommon, particularly an albino form which is primarily white with a bright orange cheek patch, and yellow crest and facial feathers. Mutants of this type are very often sterile therefore preventing further attempts at selective breeding. However, the Cockatiel owner should not despair. These birds in their normal color state may be drab in comparison with other parrots, but remember these colors represent a very unique adaptation to the special habitat conditions found in the Australian outback. We think it is far more interesting to keep captive birds which are virtually identical to their wild relatives rather than mutated freaks which may be colorful, but have been domesticated to such a degree that one can no longer appreciate the natural beauty which is the result of literally thousands of years of evolution. We know there are many who will disagree with our outlook, but we would much prefer a green, wild-type Budgerigar to a fancy product of selective breeding which might be worth a lot more.

Hybridization is a very common natural phenomenon among Australian parrot-like birds. Of the 52 species reported by Forshaw in *Australian Parrots* all but 16 are known to form hybrids. However, the Cockatiel is one of the 16! There are no reported records of cross breeding between this species and other parrots. The fact that it is the sole member of the genus *Nymphicus* and is not closely related to any other cockatoo would indicate that the prospect of interbreeding is highly unlikely.

CHAPTER ELEVEN

DEVELOPMENT OF THE CHICKS

The parents continue to sit very tightly during the first week after the eggs hatch. Again, the female assumes this duty at night and is relieved by the male at various times during the day. Once the chicks have developed a sufficient coat of feathers, which requires about three weeks, the parents progressively spend more time away from the nest during the day and huddle at the nest entrance at night.

At hatching the chicks are covered with a fluffy coat of bright yellow down. They are so light that when held in your hand the weight is barely perceptible. This is not surprising if it is remembered that adult Cockatiels weigh only about three to four ounces. The eyes of the chicks are shut at hatching and do not open until an age of about one week. The chicks are very helpless at this stage and are completely dependent on the parents for food and warmth. Birds with helpless young of this type are known as *altricial* birds and all parrots belong to this category. Some birds, such as the common Killdeer of North America are born with feathers and have the eyes open. They are able to fend for themselves almost immediately after hatching and are termed *precocial* species. Precocial birds generally have a much larger egg than altricial ones.

Unlike some other parrots, Cockatiels have a very strong parental drive and are reluctant to abandon their young in the face of danger. The Western Rosella or Stanley Parakeet is a common species found in southwestern Australia which is very sensitive to the presence of intruders. On one occasion the senior author climbed a tree to inspect a nest of eggs and although the parents were not in sight they detected something amiss on their return. The rosellas summarily flew off and never returned to their hollow which contained six eggs.

From our experiences with wild Cockatiels, the parents (particularly the female) are very reluctant to come off the nest and in some instances must be prodded. After they are disturbed they very readily return when the danger has passed and continue their nesting activities. In captivity we have observed this same sort of behavior. We do not hesitate to remove the young chicks from the nest log and handle them for brief periods. After they are returned to the nest the parents inevitably resume their care. However, we recommend a minimum of disturbance, particularly if the pair is breeding for the first or second time, or if they are nervous or relatively wild.

When handling the chicks always cradle them from below with maximum care. Even a short fall can do irreparable damage. When a chick is briefly removed from the nest it should be protected from drafts and bright sun.

The chicks begin to develop contour feathers at an age of seven to nine days. These first make their appearance in the form of prickly quills. Those of the crest, shoulder, and upper surface of the wings are the first to develop. Very gradually more feathers appear and the quills "unfold" to produce the juvenile plumage. The feathers on the cheek, throat, and tail are generally the next to develop, eventually followed by those on the back.

Throughout their development the chicks are fed periodically by the parents during the day. As their growth progresses the feedings become increasingly more frequent. Our observations of captive birds indicate that as many as 45 feedings per day may occur during the final week in the nest. The begging cries of the chicks can be heard clearly after only a few days and become more audible with increased growth. This sound consists of a sort of raspy purr followed by a rapid succession of peeps as they are fed. During the feeding process the parent bird firmly grasps the beak of the chick with its own beak and vigorously shakes its head up and down, which facilitates the movement of regurgitated food from its crop to that of the chick. As the young bird is fed its crop gradually swells until it appears as a grotesque lump at the base of the throat.

The chicks generally leave the nest at an age ranging from four to five weeks. During the last week in the nest they

A normal gray male. Photo by Brian Seed.

A normal gray female. Photo by Brian Seed.

sometimes appear at the entrance and we have occasionally seen them being coaxed towards that point by the parents, particularly the male. When they finally take their first flight they are very awkward and sometimes misjudge their landings or end up fluttering around the floor of the aviary. However, it is only a matter of a few hours before they are relatively accomplished fliers. This, of course, depends on individual birds, and some are able to fly without much difficulty on the first attempt.

Once the birds have left the nest they do not return. Instead they prefer to perch in the flight compartment or under the shelter, usually in the company of the parents, brothers, and sisters. The parents continue to feed the young Cockatiels after they leave the nest. At an age of about five to six weeks the babies begin to show an interest in seed and grasses and quickly become adept at extracting the fleshy kernels from the seed hulls. The birds are finally weaned at an age of seven to eight weeks and then can be safely removed from the parents. Cockatiels of this age are very easily tamed as pointed out in Chapter Six.

CHAPTER TWELVE

HAND REARING BABY COCKATIELS

Although we do not recommend it and prefer to leave the chicks under the care of the parents, they may be permanently removed from the nest and reared by hand. If possible it is best not to remove them until they are about seven or eight days of age, which means they should be developed to the stage where the eyes are open. They can be placed in a wooden or cardboard box. One which is about 12 inches square and 12 to 16 inches high is about right, although a slightly larger size may be utilized. The container should be kept closed with a lid at all times except when the babies are removed for feeding. A sheet of plastic over the bottom will help facilitate cleaning and it can be covered with a thin layer of sand, sawdust, or dry leaves. The droppings of the young birds are very soft and are ejected to the side of the nest box (or hollow, in nature) and for this reason it is a good idea to have the plastic sheet extend partially up the sides (it can be fastened with tape).

Until the youngsters are adequately feathered it is very important to maintain a warm temperature. We have found that a small electric heating pad placed under the box is ideal for this purpose. The pad that we use has three settings and we generally keep it on low with a folded bath towel placed between the pad and the cardboard box. If the temperature is too hot the chicks will exhibit obvious stress in the form of open mouthed panting. If this occurs the temperature must be lowered immediately. When the temperature is correct the floor of the box will be comfortably lukewarm to the touch, but not too hot.

When the chicks are under ten days old they should be fed at two to three hour intervals during the daylight hours and after dark until about 10 p.m. After ten days about every four hours will suffice (6 a.m., 10 a.m., 2 p.m., 6 p.m., 10 p.m.). We have read in various books that very young Cockatiels should be fed at regular intervals through the night, but we have never administered late night feedings and the chicks developed normally. As far as we have been able to determine they are not fed during the night by their natural parents, therefore this practice seems unnecessary. However, we usually administer the last feeding after dark before we go to bed at about 10 p.m. as it does not cause any inconvenience and the food is readily accepted.

There are many different formulas which are recommended for feeding the chicks and all are probably equally good. We have always used a relatively simple one which never fails to produce healthy birds. The basic ingredients are high protein baby cereal, powdered wheat germ, corn meal, and water. You can mix up a batch of food by combining the following ingredients:

A pair of white or albino Cockatiels. Photo by Dr. Matthew M. Vriends.

Opposite:
Opaline or pearled Cockatiels are not fixed mutations; the male (lower bird) of this pair is molting into normal gray plumage. Photo by Brian Seed.

2 cups high protein baby cereal
½ cup corn meal
¼ cup powdered wheat germ

At feeding time all that is required is a small amount of boiling water which is slowly added to several spoonfuls of the dry mixture. Enough water should be added to achieve a consistency similar to that of canned applesauce. It should not be too thick nor too runny. The formula should be allowed to cool until it is lukewarm. The temperature can be tested in the same fashion as a baby's bottle by applying a drop on the wrist. We mix the ingredients in a small plastic cup which is then floated in a pan of hot water to keep it warm while the chicks are being fed. An eye dropper with an opening of about ¼" makes a perfect feeder. The head of the chick is held securely (but not overly tight) between thumb and forefinger and the end of the eye dropper is placed in the chick's mouth, and the contents are then squeezed out slowly and steadily. Each member of the brood is given a full eye dropper and then the process is repeated several times until each crop is round and full.

The eye dropper feeder is ideal because there is very little waste and the facial feathers do not become caked with food (which always happens if a spoon is employed). When the eye dropper is utilized there is usually a little food which collects near the corners of the mouth and it should be wiped away with a tissue before replacing the chick in the nest box. If food is allowed to accumulate and dry on the facial feathers it can be difficult to remove and may result in loss of feathers and open sores. To remove caked-on dry food from these feathers you should apply warm water and very gently work it in by rubbing with your fingertips. Once the food is softened it can be wiped away with a cloth or moist sponge.

The feeding mixture which we use is sufficiently bland for feeding the smallest chicks and is also suitable for older birds up until weaning age. Weaning the young birds is a relatively simple matter. When they are about five weeks old they can be taken from the nest box and placed in a cage. At this time seed should be scattered on the floor of the cage. After a week or so the chicks will begin pecking at the seeds and from this point on their daily intake of this item will gradually increase. Once the birds begin to feed liberally on the seeds the formula feedings can be reduced to a single evening meal for about one week and then discontinued altogether.

CHAPTER THIRTEEN

DISEASE AND ILLNESSES

It is beyond the scope of this book to provide a detailed treatise on all the various ailments which may afflict captive Cockatiels. We will merely give a brief description of some of the more common ones and some not so common, but which may cause concern. For the reader who seeks more detail on this subject we would recommend a specialized book such as *Stroud's Digest on the Diseases of Birds* or *Bird Diseases* by Drs. Arnall and Keymer (available from T.F.H. Publications). Fortunately Cockatiels are extremely hardy animals and will thrive in captivity if provided with proper food and suitable accomodations. If properly cared for, the majority of birds will live out their life span without illness.

THE HOSPITAL CAGE

If your Cockatiel shows symptoms of disease it is a good practice to remove it from the company of other birds and isolate it in a special hospital cage. This will serve to prevent the disease from spreading if it is communicable and will enable you to keep the treatment process under close control. Commercial hospital cages can sometimes be purchased or can be constructed in the home workshop. Actually a makeshift one can be quickly fabricated from a normal bird cage by covering all but the front with dark plastic, heavy cloth, or a similar insulating material. The perches should be removed and the feed and water containers placed on the floor. Sick birds very often have difficulty in maintaining their normal body temperature and become easily chilled. Therefore it is important to heat the cage by either suspending a lightbulb from the top or by placing the cage on a heating pad. A very effective hospital cage can be constructed with plywood which is approximately 15 inches wide, 10 inches deep and 20 inches high. The lowermost part of the box is partitioned off with a removable piece of galvanized iron and contains three light bulbs of variable wattage (for more effective heat control). A switch for each bulb is built into a panel which covers the front of the light bulb compartment. The front of the cage is slotted to receive a piece of glass which facilitates observation and helps to conserve heat. The upper sides and top should be equipped with several circular holes covered with window screen to provide adequate ventilation. A framework covered with wire screen can be placed over the galvanized iron sheet to serve as the floor of the cage and a small perch is advisable several inches off the bottom on one side. A thermometer mounted on the back wall at perch level will help you monitor temperature conditions. The cage can be wired by an electrician for a nominal cost if your are unable to do this yourself.

Sick Cockatiels will frequently fluff out their feathers for prolonged periods which helps to conserve body heat. They are generally listless and remain perched in one position for long periods. If your bird becomes ill either place it in a hospital cage or convert its present cage into a sick bay. This should be accomplished without delay. It is important to provide warmth and to keep the bird interested in feeding. If feeding ceases the bird will weaken very quickly.

If there is doubt about the nature of the disease it will do no harm to administer a general antibiotic (such at Terramycin® , Aureomycin® , or Chloramycetin®), and in many cases the patient will undergo a quick recovery. These drugs are available from most pet shops or veterinarians and can be added to the drinking water.

NEW ARRIVALS

Cockatiels which are newly purchased should be watched closely for any symptoms of disease for the first few days.

A pair of young albino Cockatiels; these birds are sometimes called lutinos, although there is a difference between lutinos and true albinos. Photo courtesy of the San Diego Zoo.

Usually those birds which are ill can be easily detected at the pet shop or bird dealer by observing them closely. Buy only alert, active birds with a streamlined plumage. If you have purchased one or more new Cockatiels for a community aviary it is advisable to quarantine them for one week before adding them to your collection. Both quarantined aviary birds and new cage birds can be treated with an antibiotic for several days as a preventive measure. We usually give them a dose of Aureomycin® and follow the recommended dosage which appears on the label (one teaspoon per pint of drinking water).

COCKATIEL AILMENTS AND INJURIES
BROKEN LEGS:

There are two approaches to treating broken legs. . . either let nature take its course and do nothing except hospitalize and provide a good diet or apply a very lightweight splint which is lightly bandaged. If the break is below the knee (i.e., on the tibia) it is relatively easy to splint. A split quill from a larger bird such as a cockatoo or chicken makes an ideal splint. Even without special treatment broken legs will heal satisfactorily without subsequent harm to the overall health, although the bird may be permanently crippled and therefore unable to breed. For this reason we believe it is important to at least attempt the splint treatment which generally allows the bird to use the leg once it has healed. If the break occurs above the knee it will be more difficult to splint but again either a feather quill or narrow piece of plastic (cut and shaped with heat to fit the leg) will suffice. If you are uncertain about doing this job yourself the bird should be taken to a veterinarian.

During treatment it is advisable to keep the bird in a hospital cage without perches, which will help to restrict movement of the injured leg. Healing will generally occur in about two weeks and it is advisable to add an antibiotic to the drinking water during this period. Remember the bandage should be secure, but not so tight as to cut off circulation. It requires two people to apply the splint and bandage, one to hold the bird and the other to do the actual bandaging. When setting the leg it is important to have the foot and toes pointing in their normal direction, therefore it is advisable to use the healthy leg as a model.

BROKEN WINGS:

A broken wing can be set by inserting a gauze pad between the wing and the body and then securely fastening the folded wing in a comfortable, normal position against the body. This can be accomplished by using gauze bandages and adhesive tape. The bird should be placed in a very small cage, with just barely enough room to move so it will not be tempted to exercise the flight muscles. A minimum of disturbance is recommended especially if it is an aviary bird which is likely to be easily frightened. The bird can be fed and watered through the cage wires. Healing will generally be complete in two to three weeks.

COLDS:

The symptoms of a cold are similar to those for a variety of illnesses. The bird usually keeps the feathers fluffed for long periods and exhibits a marked reduction in activity. Colds are frequently accompanied by bouts of sneezing, but this behavior is not always indicative of illness. Cockatiels which are perfectly healthy very often sneeze just after scratching their head. It is a normal reaction which serves to keep the nasal passages free of debris.

If your Cockatiel seems to be suffering from a cold it is advisable to place it in a hospital cage in order to provide warmth. An antibiotic should be added to the drinking water. If the bird fails to respond to this treatment after a few days it is advisable to seek the advice of a veterinarian.

CONJUNCTIVITIS:

Birds which are afflicted with this ailment will generally blink the eyes continuously or keep them shut for long periods. The eyes will generally be very watery if examined closely. We have effectively treated this condition by isolating the bird in a hospital cage and applying Chloromycetin® eye ointment at approximately four hour intervals for several days. The ointment should be liberally applied to the surface of the eye by gently rubbing it on with your fingertip, while securely holding the bird. This medication can usually be obtained from a pet shop, pharmacy or veterinarian.

CONSTIPATION:

This condition becomes apparent when there is a lack of dropping (of course very difficult to detect in an aviary situation) and frequently the afflicted bird will repeatedly pick at the vent region with its beak. It is generally the result of a poor diet and this should be corrected at once. A very small dose of Milk of Magnesia administered with an eye dropper will help relieve the problem.

CUTS AND OPEN WOUNDS:

Open cuts and wounds, if not severe, will very quickly cease to hemorrhage and can be treated with repeated applications of antibiotic salve after being washed with hydrogen peroxide.

DIARRHEA:

This is another disorder which is frequently caused by an improper diet or from the consumption of unclean food or water. It is also a symptom which frequently accompanies a variety of illnesses. If the diet has been adequate the cause may be due to an infection and the bird should be placed on a course of antibiotic treatment in a heated hospital cage. Vitamin B12 can also be added to the drinking water (four drops per two ounces of water) during the treatment period, but should be discontinued once the droppings are normal.

EGG BINDING:

This refers to the condition in which the female Cockatiel is unable to naturally expel an egg which is lodged in the cloaca or lower oviduct. If the egg is not dislodged it prevents the passing of waste products and will result in toxemia and subsequent death. If detected in time an egg-bound Cockatiel can be effectively treated by lubricating the cloaca with several drops of lukewarm mineral or vegetable oil. This generally requires two persons, one to hold the bird in a belly up position and another to carefully apply the oil into the vent with an eye dropper. After treatment the bird should be placed in a heated hospital cage or a cardboard box placed on a warm heating pad. In most cases the egg will be passed within a few hours.

If the oil treatment fails to produce results it may be necessary to coax the egg out by applying manual pressure with the fingers. Holding the bird in a belly up position, locate the upper end of the egg and gently apply pressure to gradually force it down the oviduct toward the vent.

Egg binding can usually be avoided by providing a balanced diet supplemented with cuttlebone and a proper grit mixture.

FEATHER PICKING:

This is a relatively rare ailment among Cockatiels and is usually caused by a poor diet, particularly one lacking suitable mineral content.

FRENCH MOULT:

French moult refers to a condition in which the tail and wing feathers are continually shed resulting in a very unkempt appearance and an inability to fly (at least in a proper fashion). Birds afflicted with this malady frequently suffer a shortened life span. The exact cause of French moult is not known, but it appears to be a combination of hereditary and dietary factors. Hart (1970) gives the following advice for Budgerigars, which is also applicable to Cockatiels: *"Dipping French moult youngsters in Dett or a Lysol solution will help prevent infection and thus aid normal feather regrowth."*

GOING LIGHT:

This term is frequently used, but does not refer to a specific ailment. Rather it is a condition or symptom which may accompany other illnesses. A bird which is "going light" exhibits a marked weight loss and appears to be gradually wasting away. The recommended treatment is confinement in a hospital cage with a course of antibiotics. However, in some instances the causative agent is incurable.

HEAT STROKE:

Heat stroke is most frequently caused by careless owners who place their caged pets outdoors for extended periods without checking them. Birds placed in shaded places may be eventually exposed to direct sunlight for long periods when the sun changes positions. This danger is particularly acute if the cage is placed against or near surfaces with strong reflective properties for example on a concrete patio next to a white house. Birds suffering from severe heat stroke usually do not recover, but if the problem is detected in time the birds can be treated by spraying them with cool water or rubbing the body with a moist cloth or sponge.

INDIGESTION:

This problem will be non-existent if you adhere to the basic diet which is recommended in Chapter Three. Repeated vomiting is a sign of indigestion and if detected the diet should be corrected at once.

LICE AND MITES:

These small parasitic insects frequently live in nooks and crannies of aviary woodwork from which they make periodic forays to feed on either the blood or integument (usually feathers) of captive birds. There are various types, but all are a nuisance and should be exterminated as soon as they are detected. Infected birds will often spend a considerable amount of time scratching themselves and if they are pets the tiny mites can sometimes be seen crawling among the feathers during handling or when inspected at close range.

These pests can be eliminated with relative ease in caged birds with the use of commercial preparations available at pet shops. One popular type (which is a liquid) is applied in a thin line to the underside of perches and usually eliminates the problem in a few days. There are also various sprays which can be purchased. The latter method is recommended for aviaries. Repeated weekly applications of the insecticide may be required if the aviary is large and the problem persists. When spraying, particular attention should be given to all woodwork, nest boxes, and logs. Discuss this problem with your local pet shop owner. He has many answers!

OVERGROWN BEAK AND CLAWS:

Overgrown beaks do not appear to be particularly common among Cockatiels but if this condition occurs the beak can be periodically trimmed back to its normal length with a pair of dog toenail clippers. It is advisable to trim only a small piece at a time to avoid cutting deeply into the blood vessel which is sometimes present on the beak extension.

Overgrown claws are more common, particularly in cage birds. These can be easily trimmed with dog toenail clippers. Again it is advisable to clip small pieces at a time because of blood vessels. If bleeding occurs it will generally stop fairly quickly even if untreated, but it is advisable to clean the wound with hydrogen peroxide.

TUMORS:

Tumors occasionally appear as lumps just under the skin. A common type is yellowish in appearance. Some of these are occasionally cancerous and will eventually result in death. It is sometimes possible to remove superficial tumors, but this should only be attempted by an experienced veterinarian.

VOMITING:

As previously mentioned, this condition may be a sign of digestive disturbances due to improper diet. It may also be a sign of infection in which case it may be effectively treated by hospitalization and antibiotics.

WATERY EYES:

This is a symptom of conjunctivitis and should be treated with antibiotic ointment as prescribed above under the section dealing with this ailment.